PERFORMANCE IMPROVEMENT PROGRAMS AND EFFECTS ON JOB

PERFORMANCE

A Project Presented to the

Faculty of Spring Arbor University

in partial fulfillment of the requirements

for the degree of Master's of Science

by

Nikki Giovanni Barnett

Margaret O'Rourke-Kelly, Ph.D.

MOD T-14

July 25, 2012

Certification Page

This is to certify that the Project Thesis prepared

By: <u>Nikki Giovanni A. J. Barnett</u>

Entitled: <u>Performance Improvement Programs and Effects on Job Performance</u>

Has been accepted by the faculty of Spring Arbor University.

_____
Academic Coordinator

This Project Thesis is to be regarded as confidential and its use as a sample in future classes is restricted.

_____
Site Contact

Abstract

The purpose of this project is to construct a theoretical model that one would like to solve thoroughly by research, designing a specific plan of action for a research study and writing an extended report based on a hypothesis or research questions. This project thesis is about performance improvement programs and whether or not they increase job performance. The organization that was chosen for this project thesis was Neighborhood Health Association.

These concepts are examined empirically with quantitative methods. General business concepts are used to identify and analyze performance improvement programs and their effects on job performance. This research project discusses how PIP's will increase job performance with supporting documentation. It is worth investigating because if a cohesive bond is found between performance improvement programs, increased job performance and, employee promotions, overall positive growth of a company should form.

The initial problem within this proposal is the fact that many organizations do not take part in PIP's. It has been noted that many organizations prefer to assign duties to their current more reliable workers until they are overloaded and burnt out with various roles, assignments and duties; leaving them unable to perform at their highest ability hence no room for advancement (promotions) later. The goal of this project thesis is to examine what truly causes this. The importance of this proposal is to provide education on PIP's to improve job performance and increase managerial abilities in general.

The method of the thesis will entail the investigation of various PIP's. This will be done with research; articles, books; scholarly journals and will eventually lead to surveying. The population that will actually be sampled will consist of individual employees within and excluded from a leadership team within an organization.

Throughout the project thesis limitations will be mentioned as well as how they relate to the hypotheses. The independent and dependent variables will be discussed as well. How the sample/study was conducted will also be discussed. The sample population is the subcategory of all the research. Compounded quantitative research that stems from sampling will be distributed with questions such as:

- Could you please define the purpose of Performance Improvement Programs in your own words?
- What do you think is the primary focus of Performance Improvement Programs?
- Have you ever participated in Performance Improvement Programs?
- After completion of the Performance Improvement Program did you believe that any of the following helped improve your chances of promotion?

After the statistical analysis is complete, the approval or disapproval of the hypothesis will be determined. Existing with the data summary for conclusions; detailed research from populated fields involving PIP's must be viewed before decisions can be made and set for theory.

Table of Contents

ABSTRACT 3
CHAPTER ONE: IDENTIFICATION OF THE PROBLEM 6
HISTORY AND BACKGROUND OF THE PROBLEM 6
SCOPE OF THE PROBLEM 9
IMPORTANCE OF THE PROBLEM 10
DEFINITION OF TERMS 11
CHAPTER TWO: LITERATURE REVIEW 12
DIFFERENT VIEWS OF PERFORMANCE IMPROVEMENT PROGRAMS ..12
CHAPTER THREE: EVALUATION PLAN 24
SAMPLE POPULATION AND DATA COLLECTION 25
SWOT ANALYSIS OF PLAN 26
CHAPTER FOUR: RECOMMENDATIONS 38
MEASURING PERFORMANCE WITH RESULTS 39
SURVEY RESULTS 40
CONCLUSIONS AND RECOMMENDATIONS 44
CHAPTER FIVE: IMPLICATIONS FOR FURTHER RESEARCH 51
DEFINING RESEARCH IN-DEPTH 52
A NEW PIP PLAN 53
ORGANIZATIONAL BEHAVIOR 56
REFERENCES 63
APPENDIX A 66
SAMPLE THESIS AND PROBLEM STATEMENT 66
APPENDIX B 67
MASTER'S THESIS TOPIC PROPOSAL 67
APPENDIX C 70
REFLECTIONS 70

Chapter One: Identification of the Problem

This chapter will discuss a brief introduction to the thesis and the question of whether or not Performance improvement programs increase job performance. This section will discuss the statement of the purpose, setting of the problem, history and background of the problem, scope of the problem, and importance of the problem.

Statement of the Purpose

The purpose of this thesis asks the question do performance improvement programs (PIP's) have an effect on job performance? PIP's supposedly better the place of employment, employees, management and overall organizational morale. This project thesis will either prove or disprove the following statement: PIP's are said to help eliminate symptoms within an organization.

Setting of the Problem

The setting of the problem is within Neighborhood Health Association (NHA) located in Toledo, Ohio. Neighborhood Health Association can be described within its mission and vision statement. It is the mission of the Neighborhood Health Association to put health within reach of all community members, regardless of the ability to pay, through equal access to quality medical care and educational and support services essential for well-being of body and mind (NHA, 2009).

NHA's vision ensures access to quality medical care for anyone in need. Through effective delivery of services, Neighborhood Health Association strives to become a national model of care for the under and uninsured in our community-empowering patients through responsiveness to their needs and fostering a workplace invigorated with enthusiasm for our singular purpose. Understanding the vision and mission statement helps understand the need for the Prescription Assistance Program (NHA, 2009).

Another key aspect and vital information is stating that NHA is a 340B organization. The 340B Drug Pricing Program resulted from enactment of Public Law 102-585, the Veterans Health Care Act of 1992, which is codified as Section 340B of the Public Health Service Act. The 340B Drug Discount Program is managed by the Health Resources and Services Administration (HRSA) Office of Pharmacy Affairs (OPA).

Section 340B limits the cost of covered outpatient drugs to certain federal grantees, federally-qualified health center look-alikes and qualified disproportionate share hospitals. Participation in the Program results in significant savings estimated to be twenty to fifty percent on the cost of pharmaceuticals for safety-net providers. The purpose of a 340B Program is to utilize available federal resources. More patients are eligible and 340B helps provide more comprehensive services (HRSA, 2010).

340B guidelines are regulated by the state, federal, and national associations as well as grant providers; which is the primary source of funding for NHA. To maintain funds and receive grants it is necessary that NHA receive many audits yearly. Many of the audits are guided toward customer satisfaction. This is why the need for knowing if PIP's are a benefit or a hindrance to an organization. NHA must meet all required guidelines of the 340B Program. If all guidelines are not met they could be dismissed from funding: which in turn leads to failure of the organization.

Neighborhood Health Association is made up of the following individual locations: NHA's Administration Office or HUB, Mayores Senior Center, Mildred Bayer

Homeless Shelter, South Side Community Health Center, Cordelia Martin Health Center, Cordelia Martin Pharmacy, Cordelia Martin health Center Dental Services, Daisy Smith Pediatric Center, Neighbor Health Associations Pediatric Clinic, Huron Street Women's Health Center and Rivereast Community Health Center. All centers are located within Toledo, Ohio. Typically there is at least one center on every side of town in Toledo; North, South, East, and West.

Structuring from all the different locations come the various sub-categories or community health workers (CHW); Executive team, management team, billing team, schedulers, greeters, social services, clinical team, laboratory team, pharmacy services, dental support, medical records (EMR), WIC team, POW team, translation support services, IT department and maintenance team. NHA has such a wide range of services; performance improvement is generally a topic of discussion. With performance improvement being an issue within NHA, the CEO decided to add a quality improvement coordinator (QIC). The QIC is the executive and the leader of the quality improvement team. The QIC's goal is to have a positive effect on quality and performance improvement.

History and Background of the Problem

The initial problem to be addressed is the fact that for many centuries or longer many organizations did not take part in PIP's and was very successful. Whereas some organizations utilize PIP's present day and they fail. The importance of this thesis is to describe the role of PIP's and determine whether they help, hurt, or have no effect within an organization. This will help determine whether PIP's improved and or increase performance and managerial abilities within an organization such as NHA. Performance seems to be an issue with many organizations, but the more individuals employed within an organization the more fault is noted.

Performance has been an ongoing problem for NHA for at least a decade as of now. With several management changes, improvement efforts and ideas, all has failed thus far. It has led to an overall unmanageable turnover rate amongst employees in all departments. If it can be proven that PIP's can bring positive outcomes to an organization. With the current staff members, this may eliminate the high turnover rate. The goal is not to always fire and hire new employees. NHA wants to keep the current employees and attempt to maintain longevity and increase performance improvement. This in turn increases company morale and reflects well amongst the community and society.

Scope of the Problem

The scope of the problem and method of research for this thesis will entail the investigation of various PIP's in organizations along with a direct sample from NHA on PIP effectiveness. Sampling of roughly one hundred employees in various departments at NHA will be conducted. The sampling will include individuals whom have engaged in PIP's and individuals whom have not taken part in PIP's; all levels of the organizational hierarchy chain will be included. An estimated total number of employees average one hundred.

The dependent variable is the level of performance resulting from the PIP's. The independent variable is the PIP's. The subjects that will be sampled consist of individuals employed within NHA. The selection criteria will be reviewed for the inclusion of PIP's as well. Gender, age, and or perception could be factors for selection as well.

Importance of the Problem

The importance of the problem is to know the effects of PIPs's in regards to job performance. The general idea is to prove the hypothesis that PIP's have an effect on job performance. If this is not proven, the null hypothesis will be that PIP's do not have an effect on job performance. All of this will be decided upon completion of this thesis: Performance Improvement Programs & PIP's Effect's On Job Performance.

As stated previously this information is necessary in helping maintain the requirements for funding from state, federal and national associations. Without funding NHA being a not for profit organization; would not be able to continue existence.

Definition of Terms

This section defines the following terms that will be illustrated throughout the following thesis. The definition of terms is to provide understanding for the viewer and eliminate confusion when said terms are in use throughout various chapters.

Term	Definition
CHW	Community Health Worker
EMR	Electronic Medical Records
HRSA	Health Resources and Services Administration
HUB	Primary communication and/or networking source
ISPI	International Society of Performance Improvement
IT	Internet Technology
QIC	Quality Improvement Coordinator
NHA	Neighborhood Health Association
OB	Organizational Behavior
OPA	Office of Pharmacy Affairs
PIP	Performance Improvement Programs
PMP	Performance Management Program
POW	Perinatal Outreach Program
WIC	Special Supplemental Nutrition Program for Women, Infants and Children

Chapter Two: Literature Review

This literature review establishes a framework for the proposed questioned: Do Performance Improvement Programs (PIP's) effect job performance? This review includes various sources and information involving performance improvement programs; including job performance problems and situations that would show supporting facts in favor of and against PIP's. This review also details the need for performance improvement programs, although it does not state if or at all promotions are end results or whether PIP's helped improve chances of promotions, but it does show the impact PIP have in general positive and negative.

Performance Improvement Programs (PIP) are the continuous studies and improvements of processes, systems, and organizations. PIP's also provide data and information, in a non-punitive manner, on how well the system and process works. Implement continuing education, training programs, and equipment needs based on outcome data from the peer review performance improvement process (Department of Public Safety, 2011).

Different Views of Performance Improvement Programs

Farnsworth's found that formal management programs have increased in the past decade. Unfortunately the percentage of the increase was not given. At that time managers were more involved in self-development responsibilities. Farnsworth also states that managers need to know what aspects of current performance needs improvement and what new knowledge and skills are needed for promotion; this would be a strength taken from the article. A weakness is the fact that promotion possibilities are not mentioned (Farnsworth, 1979).

A reader is led to believe that PIP's are necessary and if knowing what knowledge and skills are needed; which would be provided during the PIP, promotional chances are increased and could be a possibility.

Brown found that performance improvement programs are viewed differently. However, this is very relevant for the literature review. Brown states that as technology streamlines within organizations, the individual management teams must learn how to expand with technology. Individuals which would indirectly be performance improvement teams have to produce results that are more effective and initiate performance improvement activities (Brown, 1998).There is a variance found in this article when compared to others mentioned in this review. The variance is the use of technological advancements leading to the need for PIP's which is noted as strength from the article. A weakness is no mentions of promotions.

The Prime II Project discusses the following overview of performance improvement, factors that affect performance, the PI process framework, considering institutional context, obtaining and maintaining stakeholder agreements, defining desired performance, describing actual performance, describing performance gaps, finding root causes, selecting and designing interventions, implementing interventions and monitoring and evaluating performance (Luoma and Voltero, 2011).

In summation of defining and describing the project it entails the mission, goals, strategies, and culture, client and community perspectives. The Prime II Project answers questions such as why did a performance gap exist, what can be done, such as possible solutions to close the gap.

Luoma and Voltero state that Performance Improvement (PI) is a method for analyzing performance problems and setting up systems. This is to ensure good performance. PI is applied most effectively within groups of workers of the same organization or those performing similar jobs (Luoma and Voltero, 2011).

An article from the (ISPI) International Society for Performance Improvement mentions providing Webinar Programs and or courses consisting of ideas, models, and tools that can be used by managers and supervisors to improve workplace performance. As a result of the webinar, individuals should be in a better position to bring performance improvement techniques to their managers and supervisors (ISPI, 2011).

The ISPI suggest another possible outcome of increased performance improvement techniques, but no mentions of promotions. The independent variable is the program itself, in which an improvement of performance resulting from the course is a positive attribute.

Harvard's performance management guidelines indicate that managing people well increases organizational effectiveness and makes them a stronger institution. Harvard also feels that what they hear from a variety of sources inside and outside of Harvard is that employees want to know how they are doing (FAS Human Resources, 2011). Harvard's performance management team believes that at its best, performance management translates into asking and listening, and that alters into a conversation. Harvard wants their managers to be clear about what they need from their employee in terms of performance and listens to what their employee tells them in terms of what he or she needs from in order to deliver results (FAS Human Resources, 2011).

Harvard's management team feels that two dissimilar advantages emerge when you keep employees informed on their performance and assist them with ways to improve. The distinctions are as follows:

1. His or her performance tends to strengthen and the employee becomes more productive. This generally renders into giving the manager more options for how you spend your time.

2. If an employee is a low performer, having a candid conversation to set clear expectations and to address any inconsistencies in performance gives you a foundation from which to address any performance issues that might follow. This effort becomes part of an organization's culture over time, and Harvard recognizes that it will take time to get where they need to be when relating performance improvements (FAS Human Resources, 2011).

Harvard is relatively in favor of PIP's. They let their management team strive from performance improvement for employees indirectly. The discussion of total quality management (TQM) surfaced when researching PIP's. TQM is also known as continuous quality improvement, continuous quality; lean and six-sigma is based upon long-term efforts to orient an organizations activity around the concept of quality. (Cummings, & Worley, 2008, p. 359) The rationale lies within the notion that quality is achieved when organizational processes produce products that meet or exceed the customers' expectations (Society for Human Resource Management, 2010).

The relative connection between TQM's and PIP's is that most PIP's depend and rely on TQM processes in hopes that employees and organizations will benefit overall as the end result. Cummings and Worley state that the overall goal of TQM is to direct the entire organization toward continuous quality improvement involving more staff than just upper level management, hence the name TQM or "continuous process improvement (Cummings and Worley, 2008, p. 359).

Michigan State University (MSU) also has a performance improvement program. MSU uses a Performance Improvement Plan form created from their performance improvement team. This form documents a plan for required performance improvement when an employee's overall performance does not meet required expectations. The form details four behavioral competencies: organizational success, making people better, job effectiveness, and additional competencies for supervisors.

The form is used to detail with specificity any and all of the areas of competencies that require attention to move one in the direction of a performance goal. It has been researched that thus far the form is advantageous to the students and workers by helping identify needed areas of improvement to move one toward various goals. This includes faculty and staff (Michigan State University, 2012).

The Community Mental Health Partnership of Southeast Michigan (CMHPSM) is an affiliation of five organizations including the Washtenaw Community Health Organization, Lenawee Community Mental Health Authority, Community Mental Health Services of Livingston County, Monroe Community Mental Health Authority, and the Washtenaw Community Supports and Treatment Service (Reitmeier, 2005).

The CMHPSM has established a Performance Improvement Program designed to assure consistently high quality services throughout the affiliation. The PIP establishes a framework for quality including accountability structure, standing committees, ad hoc teams, and performance measures. The PIP establishes processes that promote ongoing systematic evaluation of important aspects of service delivery. Any function of the affiliation can be identified for review as well (Reitmeier, 2005).

The PIP promotes ongoing improvement and replication of strengths. The PIP focuses on the delivery of services and addressing the needs of network providers and CMHPSM staff and programs. The PIP is designed to meet the needs of the partners, as well as meeting the individual organizational needs (Reitmeier, 2005).

Pioneered by Frederick Winslow Taylor scientific management populates that decisions about organizations and job design should be based on exact, scientific study of individual situations. Dessler states that training is futile if the trainee lacks the ability or motivation to benefit from it. Daft on the other hand, states that efficiency is everything.

Daft feels that this can only be done if managers develop precise, standard procedures for doing each job, select appropriate workers with adequate abilities and train workers in the standard procedures, providing performance incentives when necessary (Daft, 2007).

Neither Dessler nor Daft mentions PIP's necessity when management is training their team; they rely on the evolution of organization, theory and change.

The American Society for Training and Development (ASTD) states that PI is the process of identifying and analyzing important organizational and individual performance gaps. The ASTD believes that planning for future performance improvement, designing and developing cost-effective and ethically justifiable interventions, implementing the interventions, and evaluating the financial and non-financial results are all factors that will show positivity within an organization. Human Performance Improvement (HPI) is a growing area of expertise among workplace learning and performance professionals (ASTD, 2010).

ASTD has developed a book that they use to discuss relevant facts and information pertaining to PI. This book known as the Basics provides a guide for those with little or no background in HPI; and presents only the information one needs to know in order to be successful and gain a foothold in this important discipline. The book entails practical examples, checklists, and other tools to aid in understanding as one moves along the path to becoming a valued HPI practitioner within an organization (ASTD, 2010).

UT Dallas or The University of Texas at Dallas mentions PIP's but refers to the acronym as Performance Improvement Plan versus Performance Improvement Program. The Performance Improvement Plan (PIP) is designed to facilitate constructive discussion between a staff member and his or her supervisor and to clarify the work performance to be improved (UT Dallas, 2012).

The PIP is implemented, at the discretion of the supervisor, when it becomes necessary to help a staff member improve his or her performance. The supervisor, with input from the affected employee, develops an improvement plan; the purpose of the activities outlined is to help the employee to attain the desired level of performance (UT Dallas, 2012).

This article indicates an improvement regarding employee performance after a performance improvement plan has been implemented. Although, this PIP does not necessarily state that an actual performance improvement program has to be put in place at an organization; the PIP is more so a plan of action that a supervisor and human resources oversees and monitors.

UT Dallas makes reference to performance development planning (PDP). The PIP differs from the Performance Development Planning PDP process in the amount and quantity of the detail (UT Dallas, 2012). The PDP also elaborates on performance monitoring research (PMR). PMR is research that regularly sometimes routinely provides feedback for evaluation and control of business activity (William, Zikmund, Babin, Carr & Griffin, 2010).

Assuming an employee is already involved in a PDP process, the format and the expectation of the PIP should enable the supervisor and staff member to communicate with more specificity when involving expectations. People who are performing their jobs effectively, and meeting the expectations of the PDP process, will not need to participate in PIP's. This statement shows the necessity for PIP's and the result of improved performance (UT Dallas, 2012).

Jim Young (1994) discusses a PIP put in place for Mead Corp. Founded in Dayton, Ohio, in 1846 by Col. Daniel Mead, the company bearing his name developed into a broad-based paper organization in the first half of the twentieth century. During the 1960s, the company tried its hand at several non-paper businesses, such as coal mining, iron casting, and oil field distribution services (Young, 1994).

In 1992, Mead announced a comprehensive performance improvement program to be implemented throughout the company during the next 3 years. The company estimated that the restructuring will eliminate approximately 1,000 staff and management positions and result in annualized savings of sixty million dollars.

The Mead PIP consisted of closing performance gaps in surface print improvement, product availability, and consistency. There were many delivery issues as well that would undergo construction with the PIP implementation (Young, 1994). The main focus of this PIP for Mead is not based on improvement of the employees and job performance; it is solely based on production and output improvement. The Mead article demonstrates a need for PIP but again, is not necessarily related to job performance for individuals; it is based upon production.

Texas Medical Association (TMA) has a PIP as well. Their Performance Improvement Programs also known as Pay for Performance, P4P or value-based purchasing are payment models that reward physicians, hospitals, medical groups, and other health care providers for meeting certain performance measures for quality and efficiency. Rising health care costs have brought this payment model to the forefront of health care reform (Texas Medical Association, 2011).

TMA is working with other health care stakeholders to improve the validity of quality indicators, respect patient and physician autonomy and privacy, and reduce administrative burdens that may be associated with such programs (Texas Medical Association, 2011). With the information provided PIP's are necessary to move toward healthcare reform and reward staff at TMA.

Meta-analytic research conducted by the Corporate Executive Board (2004) found that PMP's differ slightly from PIP's. Performance Management Programs consists of a set of management and analytic processes that enable the management of an organizations performance to achieve one or more pre-selected goals (Corporate Executive Board, 2004).

The Corporate Executive Boards research states that even though organizations reported few problems implementing PMP's; challenges surfaced such as concluding an agreement on the relevancy and competency to particular business environments, clarifying competencies describing peoples actions and not necessarily their jobs and defining processes for assessing individuals against models (Corporate Executive Board, 2004).

The meta-analysis cites studies where employees and managers reported being "somewhat satisfied" or "not satisfied" with their organizations performance management system (Corporate Executive Board, 2004). Areas of dissatisfaction include employee development-related components such as providing the basis for career and development planning.

The relevance and strength found within the research helped show the need for performance improvement programs. The Corporate Executive Boards statement of organizations moving away from PIP's is relevant. There is no need for performance management programs if there is a problem with employees involving careers and development planning. If the initiations of performance improvement programs are implemented prior to the performance management programs, then there may actually be a need for PMP's. Improvement should be implemented prior to management, thus leading to the increased chances for promotion.

Mark Crowell Consulting mentions that Mark Crowell himself has led performance improvement teams for close to two decades, starting by facilitating quality circles and TQM teams for Prudential Healthcare in the early nineties. The foundation of Crowell's work is the model of improvement described in The Improvement Guide: A Practical Approach to Enhancing Organizational Performance, 1996 (Mark Crowell Consulting, 2008).

The guide is endorsed by the Institute for Healthcare Improvement as a successful model. This complements other change models and serves to accelerate improvement efforts. At the core of the improvement model is the Plan-Do-Study-Act (PDSA) cycle, which originated in the work of Walter A. Shewhart and was later adapted by W. Edwards Deming (Mark Crowell Consulting, 2008).

All projects are managed utilizing the well-tested principles that anchor effective performance improvement: high involvement of persons actually doing the work, the use of performance metrics to gauge the impact of changes, a bias toward implementing small, repeated tests of change to realize success. What sets Mark's work apart from others is explicit attention and response to the cultural dynamics that must be recognized and accommodated in order to implement change successfully. Strategies of reinvigoration are integrated into project deliverables, to ensure that improved performance is sustained over time (Mark Crowell Consulting, 2008). Marks results show a need for PIP's within an environment. His information also supports performance improvement as well.

Conclusion

Concluding the literature review, there are many instances of the problem as it is reviewed in several settings where the reference material helps support the fact that performance improvement programs do indeed increase or has an impact on job performance. However, it appears that a negative factor would be concluding whether or not PIP's are directly related to job performance and or if they pertain to employees in general verses a product or company as a whole entity.

A new avenue for consideration is the discussion of Performance Improvement Plans verses Performance Improvement Programs and the difference amongst the two. Chapter three will discuss realistic possible solutions and facts as to whether PIP's do indeed increase job performance or what alternative outcomes are found when using PIP's.

Chapter Three: Evaluation Plan

This chapter is to discover all possible outcomes that could result from using PIP's. Performance Improvement Programs (PIP) are the continuous study and improvement of process, system or organization. PIP's also provide data and information, in a non-punitive manner, on how well the system and process works.

PIP's supposedly better the place of employment, employees, management and overall organizational morale. PIP's are said to help eliminate symptoms within an organization. A comprehensive evaluation plan has been constructed and discussed in depth.

Several different outcomes and alternatives will be discussed in regards to whether or not PIP's increase job performance, and if not what other outcomes could result from PIP's. The following outcomes of PIP's will be broken down in SWOT analysis; strengths, weaknesses, opportunities, and threats of using PIP's. Table 1.1 is an example of the research layout that coincides with the survey and sampling.

Table 1.1 Example Research Layout (Survey & Sampling)

```
                    SAMPLE DESIGN
                   /              \
        PROBABILITY SAMPLING    NON-PROBABILITY SAMPLING
              |
        DATA COLLECTION
              |
        EDITING & CODING DATA
                    |
              DATA PROCESSING & ANALYSIS
                            |
                    INTERPRETATIONS OF FINDINGS
                                    |
                                  REPORT
```

The method of research or evaluation plan for this proposal will entail the investigation of various PIP's. The facts for the overall evaluation of PIP's will be provided from survey responses or sampling. Subjects will consist of graduates and non-graduates of PIP's from all fields of study.

Sample Population and Data Collection

The sample will be the subcategory of all the research from the introduction of the proposal, the statistical analysis to be calculated with results in chapter four, the end results to support the hypothesis and the overall discussion of the hypothesis, proposal and situation at hand. The subjects will total fifty to one-hundred. Figure 1.2 is an example of the survey letter used to collect data and build an analysis. Figure 1.3 illustrates the survey questions used.

The data collection methodology includes a self-developed survey that will be distributed randomly. All questions are multiple choices. Only one answer may be selected per question and all questions must be answered for the data to be included in the study. In-house editing will be done to investigate the data. Computerized survey data processing will be used as well but the field edit will check for errors.

Questions one through five is demographic questions and will help determine if there is specificity in demographics that relates to the outcome of the study or the hypotheses. The remaining four questions relate solely to Performance Improvement Programs, job performance, and promotions are a true outcome and or benefit from the program. Please see Figure 1.1 for further details of the data analysis.

The analysis is conducted using the percent and chi-square method. A Chi-Squared analysis consist of adding up all of the survey results and breaking them down into percent categories based upon each question asked and answered correctly. Chi-Squared tests hypotheses stating that the frequency distribution of certain events observed in a sample are consistent with a particular theoretical distribution. The chi-square distribution is used in the common chi-square tests for goodness of fit (Balakrishnan, Johnson & Koltz, 1994).

The data analysis will be performed based upon the most recent information a subject has pertaining to Performance Improvement Programs. A limitation of the data collection process is the fact that some of the data may be biased. Although everything is multiple choices, some questions have "not applicable" boxes or "other" boxes and the surveyor is asked to write personal responses to the question. If too many hand written responses are given, it will become difficult to calculate data and come to a conclusion based upon the survey responses. This may lead to a null hypothesis depending on responses given.

SWOT Analysis of Plan

A breakdown of the SWOT analysis is used to determine possible strengths, weaknesses, opportunities, and threats of using PIP's. SWOT analysis is a strategic planning method used to evaluate the strengths, opportunities, weaknesses and threats involved in a project or in a business venture; such as PIP. It involves specifying the objective of the business venture or project and identifying the internal and external factors that are favorable and unfavorable to achieve that objective. Figure 1.5 illustrates the breakdown of SWOT analysis plans.

Strengths that could result from using PIP's of course are performance improvements amongst employees. That is first and foremost the most influential strength of all. Other areas of improvement could be attitude, leadership, team building, and any aspect to enhance the ability of one to perform his or her job adequately and without direction from a direct supervisor.

A weakness that could result from the use of PIP's would be no positive results and the PIP is costly to the organization. Not only does cost become a factor but also time, it takes many hours, days and months to initiate plan and implement PIP. Much PIP's cost organizations thousands of dollars, and money wasted is always a weakness.

An opportunity that could develop from the use of PIPs could be positivity from the outcome of the PIP's and by what is known as word of mouth many other may want to use similar PIP's within their organizations.

Another opportunity could be that the PIP was beneficial and many individuals did gain from it. This leads to performance enhancements and possibly promotions for many employees. A lot of organizations budgets limits promotions so as an alternative employees could have the option of team leading, organizing or even taking on more responsibilities to add to their history and background if pay increases are unavailable.

Threats of using PIP's are straight forward, just as the PIP came into place not that long ago, another program can easily replace it. The acronym alone started as PIP which represented Performance Improvement Program. From then to now the acronym has gained another name which stands for Performance Improvement Plan (PIP). This just shows how another plan or program can take the place of a previous one if not successful enough.

A Performance Improvement Plan (PIP) is used when you have identified a performance problem and are looking for ways to improve the performance of an employee. The Performance Improvement Plan plays an integral role in correcting performance discrepancies. It is a tool to monitor and measure the deficient work products, processes and or behaviors of a particular employee in an effort to improve performance or modify behavior.

There are quite a few steps in order to follow through with a Performance Improvement Plan verses a Performance Improvement Program (Indiana State University, 2012). Of course the initiator of either program has strict guidelines and rules to abide by but the plan has steps which were found when researching information found on Indiana University's website regarding Performance Improvement Plans. Figure 1.4 illustrates the steps to a performance improvement plan. These steps have been provided by Indiana State University.

One example of how threats can enter any environment, in this case the performance improvement plan has taken the place of the program itself. Research indicates many programs such as both this one that will eliminate or make it hard for performance improvement programs to excel. What these programs consist of is basically self-motivation and there are a lot of programs current day owned by independent contractors looking to improve quality at a place of employment. The goal is to make sure Performance Improvement Programs remain number as the option for improvement and the rest become obsolete over time.

Conclusion

Survey results will help determine whether or not PIP's are effective and beneficial. The data gathered will not be able to determine whether or not other alternatives to PIP's are better or worse, the goal is to determine whether or not PIP's are beneficial or a hindrance to an organization. The survey results will be discussed in chapter four.

Figure 1.1 Data Analysis

Hypotheses	Independent Variables	Dependent Variable	Scoring
Performance Improvement Programs increasing job performance.	Performance Improvement Programs Performance Management Programs Performance Improvement Plan	Promotions Outcomes other than promotions such as leadership roles & duties, self-development	Chi-Squared Test for goodness
Questions	Demographic Questions	Study Questions	PIP Related Questions
Multiple Choice Text Box Comments	Gender	Multiple Choice Free Text Answers	Purpose of PIP's
	Age		Participation in PIP's
	Field		Primary focus of PIP's
	Experience		What influenced chances of promotion after completion of PIP
	PIP Participant		Better performance after PIP's at work
	Define PIP		Explaining benefits of PIP's

Figure 1.2 Example Survey Letter

Greetings:

I am Nikki Barnett and I am currently enrolled in the Masters Program (Management & Organizational Development) at Spring Arbor University. I am conducting this survey for my thesis and your input is needed and will be greatly appreciated.

This survey is being provided to you in attempt to answer the question: Do Performance Improvement Programs (PIP's) increase job performance? This survey is being distributed as a random sample via email. This is a multiple choice survey and ALL of the questions must be answered in order for your input to be calculated properly.

The survey responses, your answers to the questions will only be used for the study and will not be distributed with any personal demographics. This is not related to your employer, performance or personal characteristics.

Spring Arbor University has authorized the production of this survey for my research study and solely for the purpose of assisting with the completion of my thesis. If results are published, consent will be required from you before any information can be released.

If you have any questions regarding this survey, please feel free to contact me at ni321772@arbor.edu

Thank You.

Nikki Giovanni Barnett, RHIT, CPhT, MSM

By initialing the box below and returning this form via email I am stating that I am willing to participate in this survey and am allowing the results to be used for research purposes only.

☐ ← Initial Here

Please click reply, scroll down and initial the box, then send the message back to me. Once your consent has been submitted, please return to the original message and click the link below to complete the survey. Thank you for your time.

http://www.surveymonkey.com/s/JPTR7CK

Figure 1.3 Survey Questions

1. Please state your gender.

○ Male

○ Female

2. Please state your age.

○ 18-23

○ 24-29

○ 30-35

○ 36-41

○ 42-46

○ 47-51

○ 52-57

○ 58-63

○ 64+

3. Please state your field.

○ Healthcare

○ Medical

○ Marketing

○ Agriculture

○ Transportation

○ Administration

○ Pharmaceuticals

○ Factory/Warehouse/Production

○ Data Entry

○ Clerical

○ Other

_____

4. How many years of experience do you have in your field?

○ 0-3

○ 4-6

○ 7-10

○ 11-13

○ 14-17

○ 17+

5. Please define the purpose of Performance Improvement Programs in your own words.

_____

6. Have you ever participated in Performance Improvement programs?

○ Yes

○ No

If yes what year:

_____

7. What do you think is the primary focus of Performance Improvement Programs?

○ Job Satisfaction

○ Waste of Time and Money

○ Increase Chances of Promotion

○ Overall Morale

○ Increased Performance

○ Increase Customer/Patient Satisfaction

○ I don't care

8. After completion of the Performance Improvement Program did you believe that any of the the following helped improve your chances of promotion?

○ Gender

○ Years of Experience

○ Other

○ No Promotion due to performance Improvement Program

○ Not Applicable

○ Age

○ Increased Job Performance as a Result from the Performance Improvement Program

○ Did Not Complete the Program

9. Do you feel that Performance Improvement programs help you perform better at work?

○ Yes

○ No

○ Yes, but not at work

10. Would you say that Performance Improvement Programs are beneficial in any of the following ways? Select all that may apply:

○ Less Stress

○ Communication Skills

○ Job performance

○ Customer Service Skills

○ Production

○ Mentally

○ Physically

○ Emotionally

○ Financially

○ Other

If other benefits please detail below:

_____

Figure 1.4 Performance Improvement Plan

<u>Indiana State University</u>

1. Define the problem. This is the deficiency statement. Determine if the problem is a performance problem (employee has not been able to demonstrate mastery of skills/tasks) or a behavior problem (employee may perform the tasks but creates an environment that disrupts the workplace).

2. Define the duties or behaviors where improvement is required.

    a. What are the aspects of performance required to successfully perform these duties?

    b. Which skills need improvement?

    c. What changes need to be made in application of skills an employee has already demonstrated?

    d. What behaviors need modified?

3. Establish the priorities of the duties.

    a. What are the possible consequences of errors associated with these duties?

    b. How frequently are these duties performed?

    c. How do they relate when compared with other duties?

4. Identify the standards upon which performance will be measured for each of the duties identified.

    a. Are they reasonable?

    b. Are they attainable?

5. Establish short-range and long-range goals and time tables for accomplishing change in performance/behavior with employee.

a. Are they reasonable?

   b. Are they attainable?

6. Develop an action plan.

   a. What will the manager do to help the employee accomplish the goals within the desired time frame?

   b. What will the employee do to facilitate improvement of the product or process?

   c. Are the items reasonable?

   d. Can the items be accomplished?

   e. Are the items flexible?

7. Establish periodic review dates.

   a. Are the employee and the manager both aware of what will be reviewed at each of these meetings?

8. Measure actual performance against the standards to determine if expectations were:

   a. not met

   b. exceeded

9. Establish a Performance Improvement Plan file for the employee.

   a. Does the file contain documentation which identifies both improvements and/or continued deficiencies?

   b. Is the employee encouraged to review this file periodically?

10. Put the Performance Improvement Plan in writing.

    a. Has plain and simple language been used?

    b. Have specific references been used to identify areas of deficiency?

c. Have specific examples been used in periodic reviews which clearly identify accomplishments or continuing deficiencies?

d. Have you chosen an easy-to-read format such as a Figure or a duty by duty listing?

e. Have the Terms of Agreement been included in the Performance Improvement Plan?

Figure 1.5 SWOT Analysis Diagrams

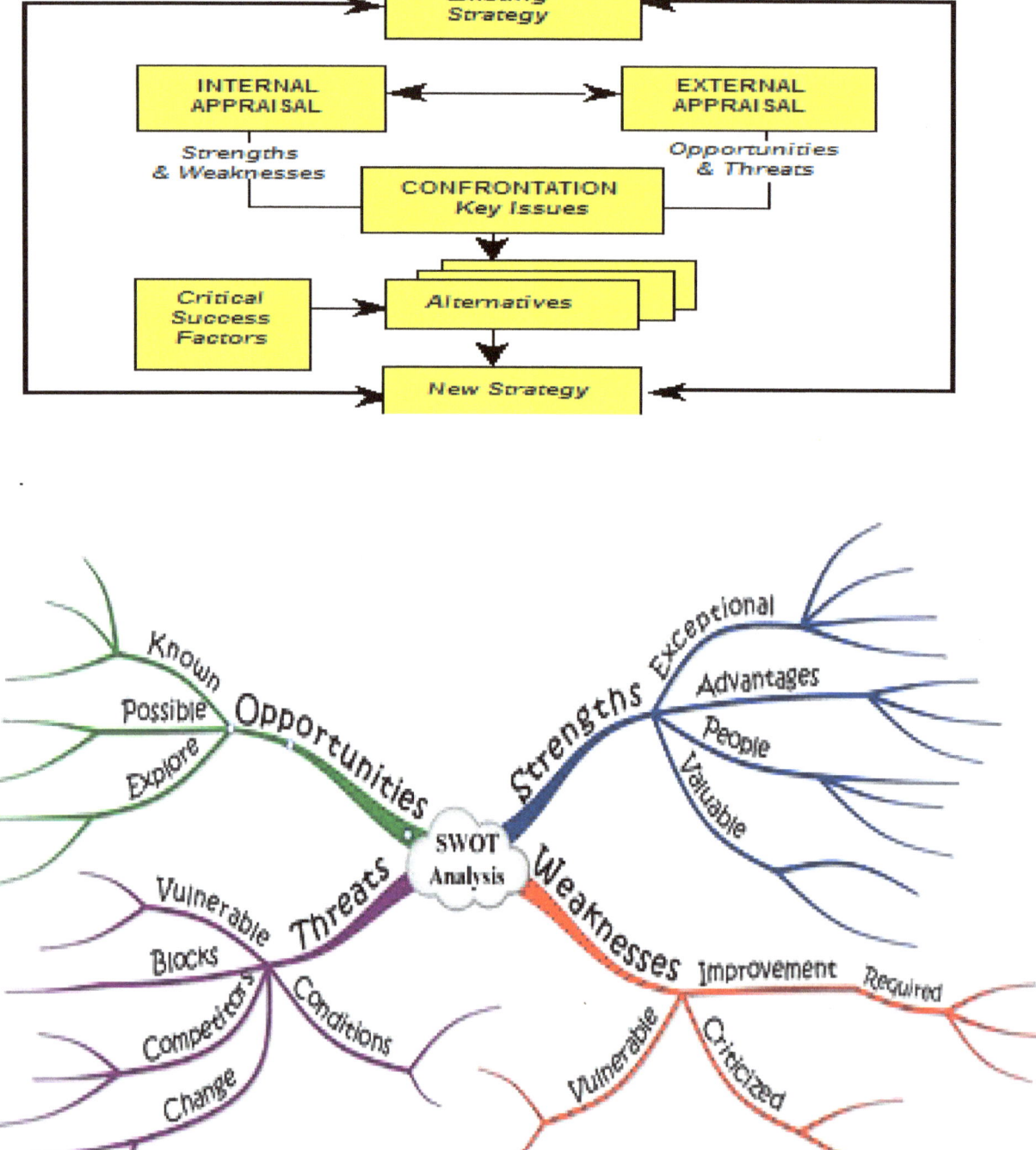

Chapter Four Recommendations

This chapter explores the results obtained from the investigation of the thesis project. The hypothesis in question was whether or not performance improvement programs increase or improve performance in the workplace. Concepts that are applicable to the problem have been examined and the data has been calculated. It has been determined from the study results regarding PIP's and the increase in job performance is null and void. Relating these findings to the study in question; PIP's do not increase job performance.

Measuring Performance with Results

Performance is a measure of the results achieved. Performance efficiency is the ratio between effort expended and results achieved. The difference between current performance and the theoretical performance limit is the performance improvement zone (ASTD, 2010).

Another way to think of performance improvement is to see it as improvement in four potential areas. First, is the resource input requirements; examples being reduced working capital, material, replacement or reorder time, and set-up requirements. Second, is the throughput requirements, often viewed as process efficiency; this is measured in terms of time, waste, and resource utilization. Third, output requirements, often viewed from a cost/price, quality, functionality perspective. Fourth, outcome requirements, did it end up making a difference (ASTD, 2010).

Performance is an abstract concept and must be represented by concrete, measurable phenomena or events to be measured. Performance assumes an actor of some kind but the actor could be an individual person or a group of people acting in concert. The performance platform is the infrastructure or devices used in the performance act (ASTD, 2010).

Survey Results

There are two main ways to improve performance: improving the measured attribute by using the performance platform more effectively, or by improving the measured attribute by modifying the performance platform, which in turn allows a given level of use to be more effective in producing the desired output (ASTD, 2010).

According to the study survey results almost ninety-five percent of the sample population; which was Neighborhood Health Association, all stated that PIP's do not increase the possibility of promotions nor do they enhance job performance. The survey itself left various text boxes for individuals to fill in their own responses and the majority of the responses stated that PIP's were not a helping aid. According to the study population, performance improvement resides in the foundation of the organization.

Many of the text boxes suggest that the upper management team plays a major role in performance improvement and if the management team lacks the necessary performance qualities that they need to keep their staff members engaged in quality improvement overall, then a program for employees is not the solution; the solution would be to hire the appropriate managers that possess the necessary skills to keep their team motivated in performance improvement.

To discuss the findings in detail, one hundred surveys were distributed to the employees at Neighborhood Health Association. This included all employees, including the management teams. The only exclusive individuals are the CFO, whom was terminated, the fill in CEO, whom was overwhelmed and the CEO whom stated she did not have time to participate in the study. She did however grant permission for the study to be conducted.

Out of one hundred surveys sixty-three surveys were received with all necessary actual data complete; many with additional text box information. Twenty-four of the surveys received were simply email responses detailing why individuals did not want to participate in the survey after reading the survey questions. These twenty-four individuals decided to give actual information as to why they felt PIP's not beneficial and what could be done to improve performance.

Ten surveys were incomplete; therefore were thrown out as well as the three surveys that individuals did not respond to. The assumption has been made that the three non-responsive surveys were individuals whom did not want to participate nor give feedback regarding NHA and PIP's. Tables 1.2 through Tables 1.12 detail the survey responses with the necessary data calculations.

Connecting completed survey results with written responses all of the employees at NHA feel that PIP's are unnecessary and are not beneficial for performance improvements for their place of employment. However, question number nine found on Table 1.11 asks the following question: Do you feel that Performance Improvement programs help you perform better at work? The answer to this question shows that thirty-three of the respondents stated no, zero of the respondent's state yes and thirty of the respondents stated yes, but not at work.

This shows a difference of opinion for the study concluding that the sample population feels that PIP's possibly are beneficial; just not at NHA.

Survey responses suggest that NHA needs to be restructured. Mentions of treating employees like actual people; being concerned with death of loved ones, personal family issues especially of employees whom have been with the company five or more years and usually have no issues with attendance, tardiness and disciplinary actions need to be treated with respect when an emergency situation arises.

The survey responses via email stated that it is the poor management from the upper management team including the CEO and the loss of the CFO that has caused the employee morale to drop. Organizational morale refers to the way people feel about their jobs and the organization they work for. It includes the atmosphere of the workplace, the way people work together as a team, and their general level of confidence and satisfaction. For example, an organization with high morale would have a busy, but positive atmosphere, where everyone knew what was expected and worked well together to meet these common goals. High organizational morale usually leads to happy workers and financial success (UT Dallas, 2012).

Low morale, on the other hand, can be a wildly destructive force. It can reduce productivity, harm relationships with clients and customers, and, ultimately, destroy the organization's bottom line. Many different things can trigger low organizational morale. Layoffs and job insecurity are among the most obvious. But, morale problems can also come from poor communication between managers and workers, hard work not being recognized or rewarded, or even missed opportunities for employees to socialize and bond with one another. An organization with low morale must move quickly and decisively to fix the problem before it is out of control. For the most part, it is up to the managers and other senior staff to implement strategies that will fix the problem. However, the average worker does have some influence over improving morale (UT Dallas, 2012).

One surveyor mentioned that everyone wants to feel involved and important to the success of the organization. It is important that companies demonstrate their trust in their workforce by allowing employees to provide input, and help with decision-making related to their jobs. If the organization doesn't do this, Employees could suggest they develop problem-solving teams to work on particular issues, or even something as simple as a suggestion box that would allow people to make comments on improving performance. The more confidence an organization shows in its workers, the more confident and productive they will be.

Another surveyor mentioned that in any workplace, managers need to treat each employee as an individual, and recognize their hard work and contributions to the organization. Many good employees leave their jobs because they simply haven't received meaningful feedback on how they are doing, or the recognition they feel they deserve. It is important that an organization recognize each person's contribution to the company. This doesn't need to be a big gesture or cash prize. It is the recognition that counts not the reward.

If employees feel their workplace could benefit from some kind of employee recognition program, they should suggest it to a superior. Some companies institute a "penny prize," where employees are given a penny as a reward for their contribution to the company (UT Dallas, 2012). The amount of the reward is not important, being recognized in front of the entire staff for your achievements is. No one wants to work in an environment where people are unhappy, stressed out or feel they can't make a difference. While it may seem it is the boss's job to keep the workers happy, everyone can have a hand in improving morale and making their organization a great place to go to work.

Lastly, relating morale to NHA, the survey respondents state that their performance would improve naturally if employees actually felt as if they were a part of a team or at least a real member (person) within the organization.

The survey results also suggest that there is a possibility that the respondents didn't exactly answer the PIP's questions adequately based on the assumption that all comments were negatively geared toward NHA. It is possible with the same survey sample (population) in a different environment the study survey answers could have differed and shown an increase in performance; as the result of PIP's NHA has a negative impact on this study.

Conclusions and Recommendations

Conclusions and recommendations that result from the research study as implied from the written comments via email suggest that PIP's are not the issue; being beneficial or non-beneficial. The problem is NHA. A good conclusion would be to suggest conducting this study using another organization other than NHA. This will be discussed in detail in chapter five.

Table 1.2 Survey Study Overview of Participants

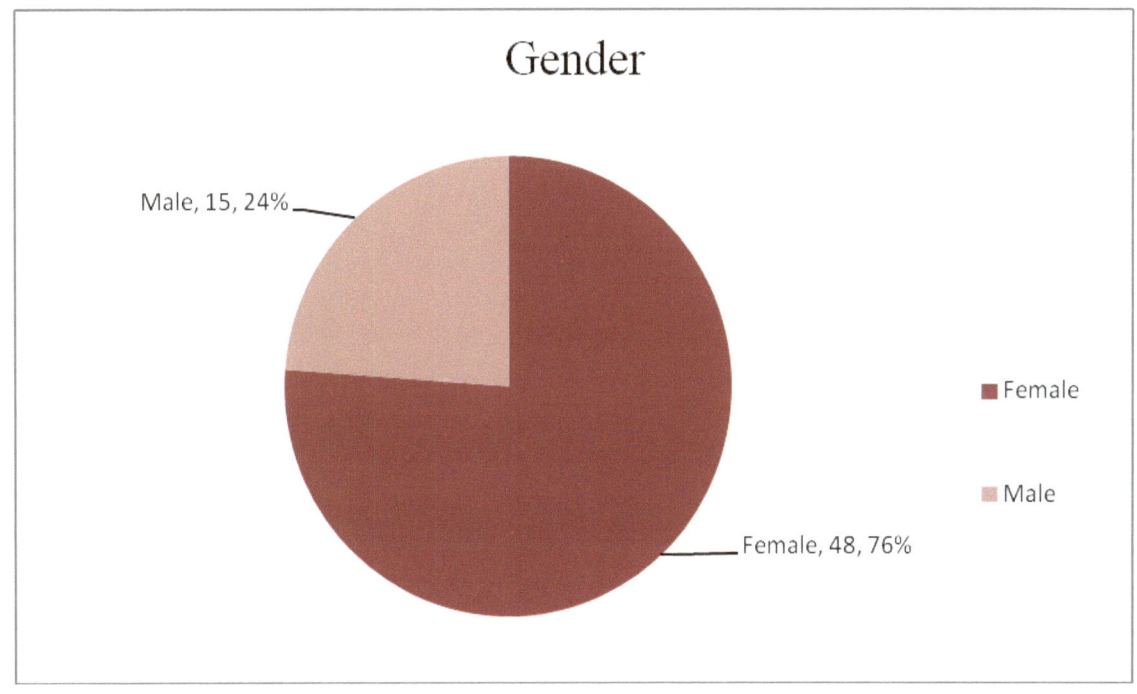

Table 1.3 Question One: Gender

Table 1.4 Question Two: Age

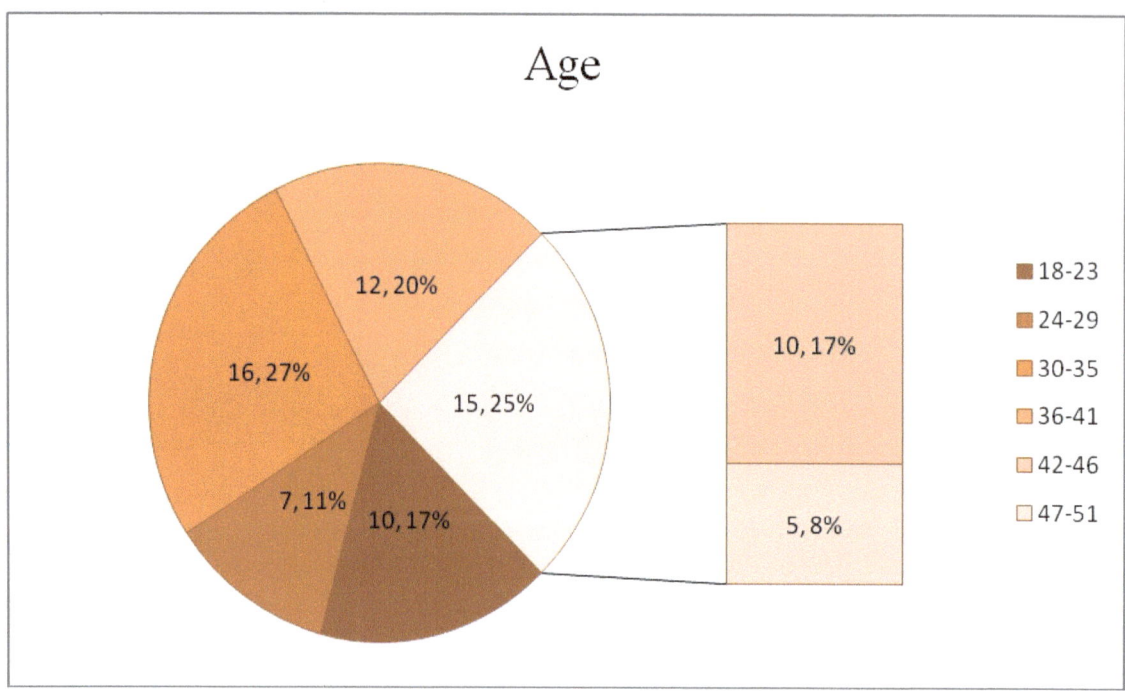

Table 1.5 Question Three: Professional Field

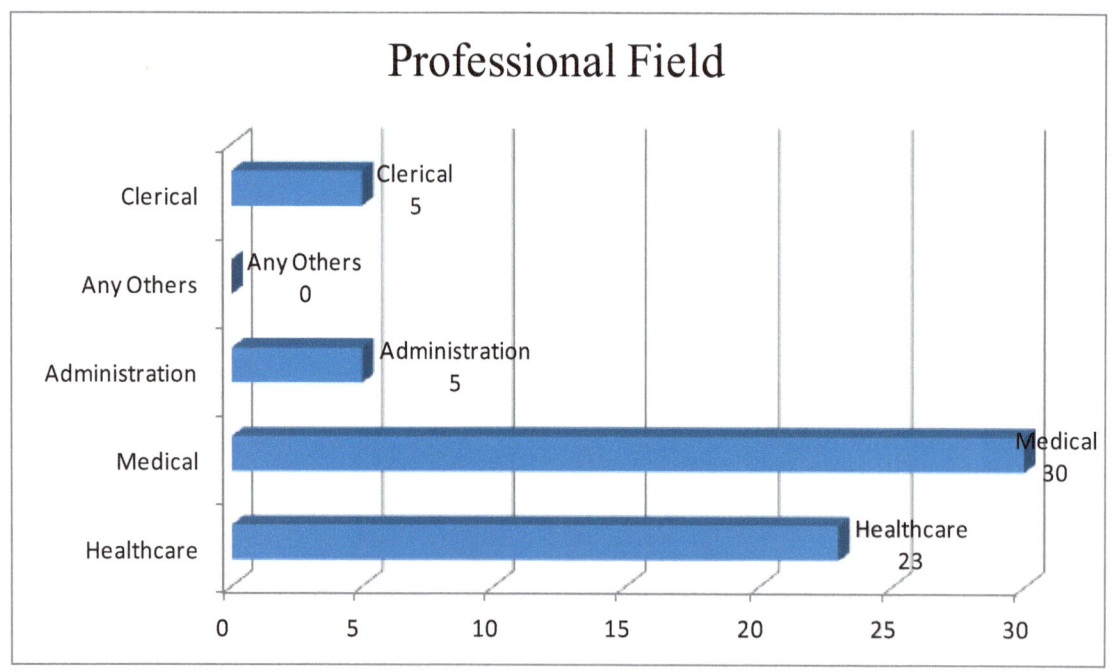

Table 1.6 Question Four: Years of Experience

Table 1.7 Question Five Definition of PIP (Own Words)

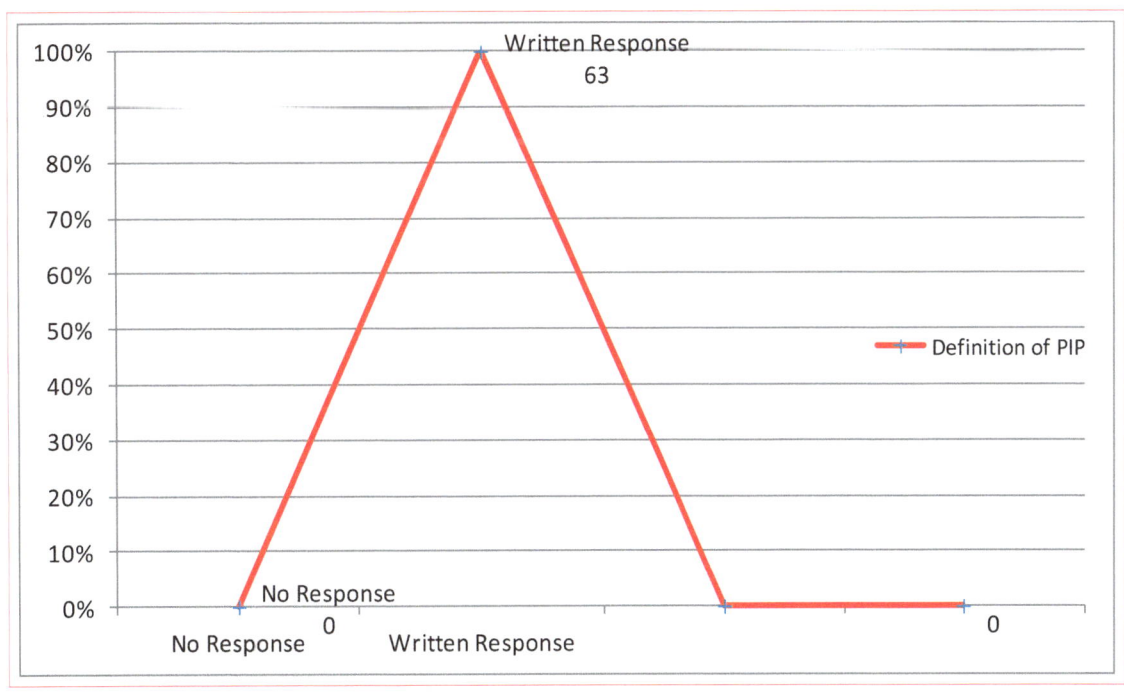

Table 1.8 Question Six: Previous PIP Participant

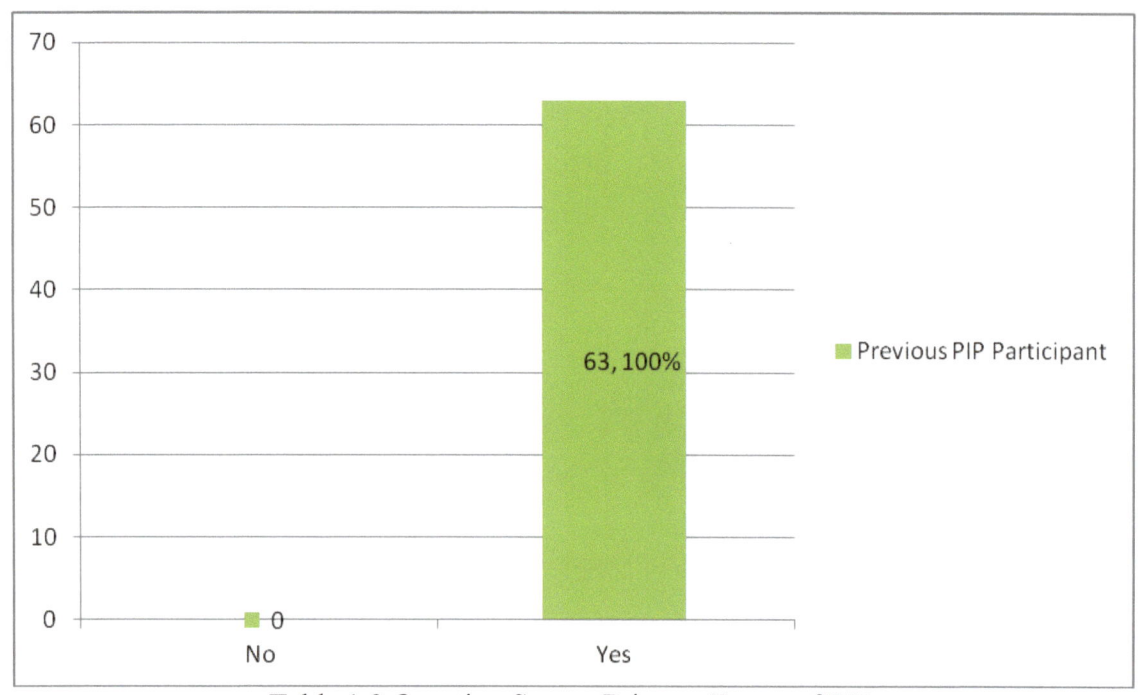

Table 1.9 Question Seven: Primary Focus of PIP

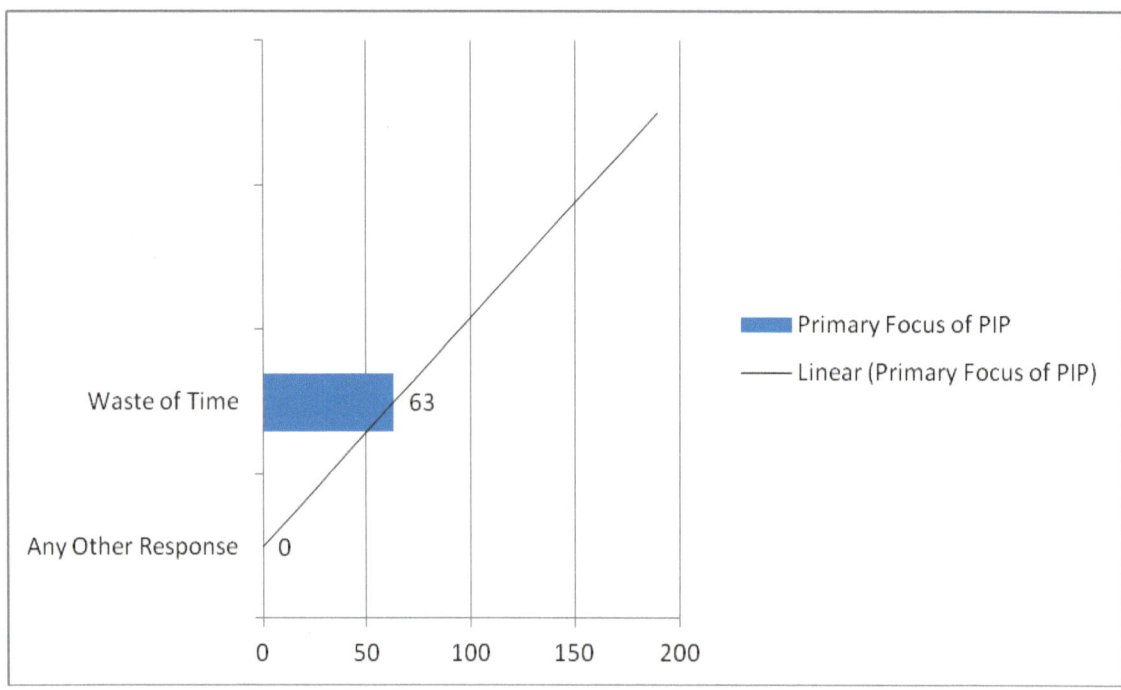

Table 1.10 Question Eight: Upon Completion of PIP, Promotional Possibilities

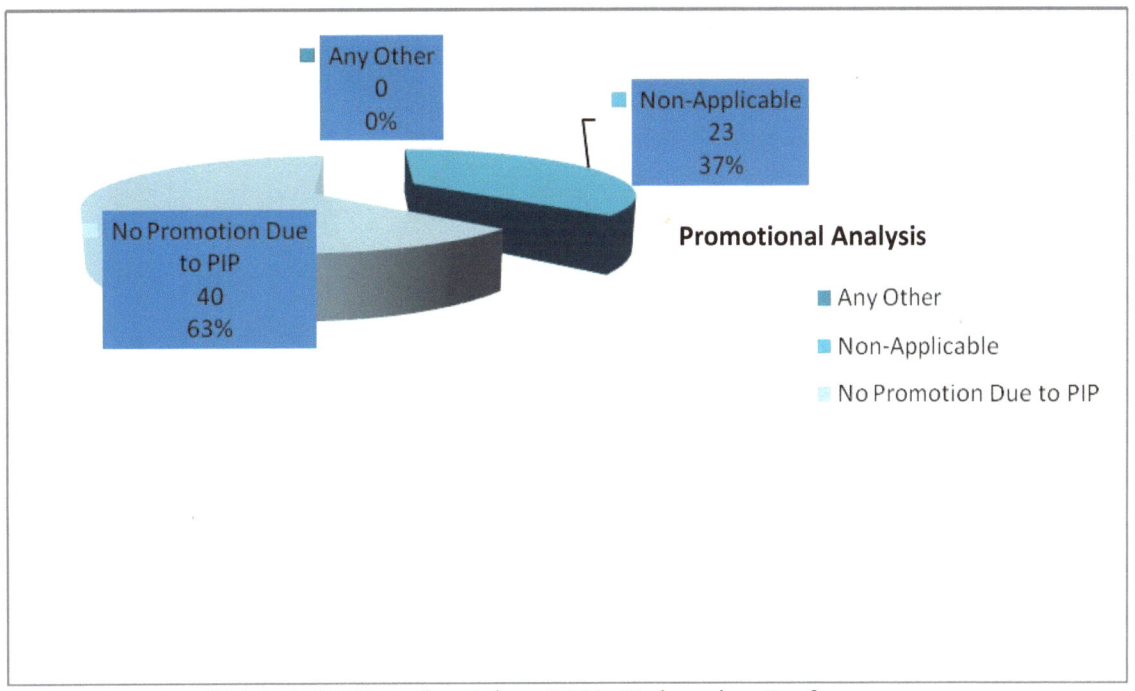

Table 1.11 Question Nine: PIP's Enhancing Performance

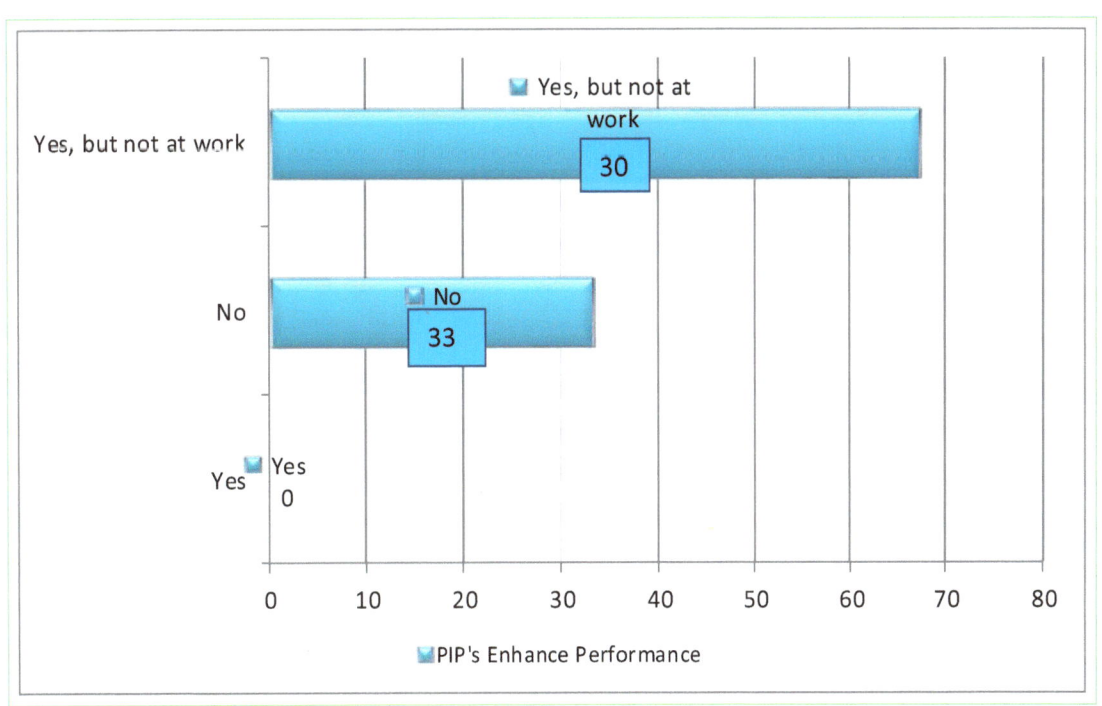

Table 1.12 Question Ten: PIP's Being Beneficial in Any Way

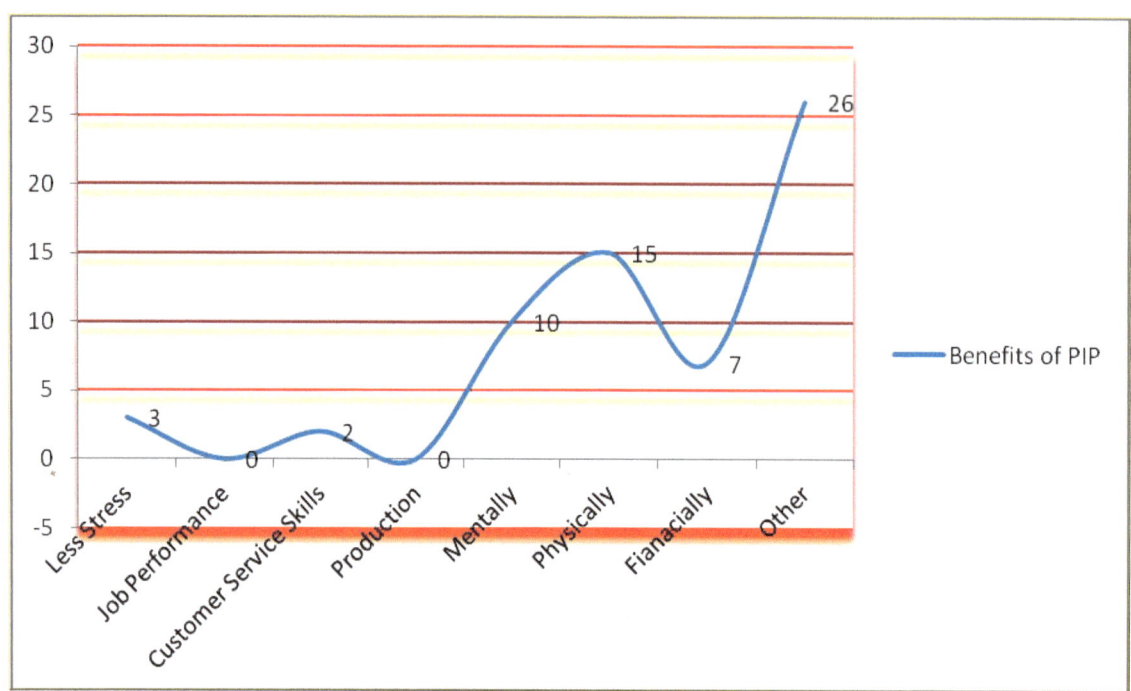

Chapter Five: Implications for Further Research

This chapter will discuss and present possibly a new direction for the research study. It will give an idea of where PIP's and its relations with performance improvement is headed, whether the study should be repeated with additional and further research, and or altered to have more beneficial future results.

Generally, just as the original study research is understood to follow a certain structural process. The following steps will be used for further research and are as follows: formation of the topic, hypothesis, conceptual definitions, and operational definitions, gathering of data, analysis of data, test or revising of the hypothesis and the conclusion and iteration if necessary.

A common misunderstanding is that by this method a hypothesis can be proven or tested. Generally a hypothesis is used to make predictions that can be tested by observing the outcome of an experiment. If the outcome is inconsistent with the hypothesis, then the hypothesis is rejected. However, if the outcome is consistent with the hypothesis, the experiment is said to support the hypothesis.

This careful language is used because researchers recognize that alternative hypotheses may also be consistent with the observations. In this sense, a hypothesis can never be proven, but rather only supported by surviving rounds of scientific testing and, eventually, becoming widely thought of as true or better, predictive, but this is not the same as it having been proven (UT Dallas, 2012).

A useful hypothesis allows prediction and within the accuracy of observation of the time, the prediction will be verified. As the accuracy of observation improves with time, the hypothesis may no longer provide an accurate prediction. In this case a new hypothesis will arise to challenge the old, and to the extent that the new hypothesis makes more accurate predictions than the old, the new will supplant it (Dictionary.Com, LLC, 2012).

After explaining a hypothesis in depth the outcome of the original research is inconsistent with the hypothesis, therefor the hypothesis has been rejected in total. This rejection has been made with regards to the organizations (NHA's) structure and employees being a vital factor causing or forcing the rejection. Over half of the data was null and void as it pertains to the hypothesis of performance improvements due to the negativity that stemmed from the employees toward NHA with no regards to PIP's whatsoever.

Defining Research In-Depth

Research is said to have human activity based on intellectual application in the investigation of matter (UT Dallas, 2012). The primary aim for applied research is discovering, interpreting, and the development of methods and systems for the advancement of human knowledge on a wide variety of scientific matters of our world and the universe. Research can use the scientific method, but need not do so. In this case seeking a new direction for the study, a basic research method with a scientific approach will be used.

Basic research, also known as fundamental or dumb research has as its primary objective the advancement of knowledge and the theoretical understanding of the relations among variables. It is exploratory and often driven by the researcher's curiosity, interest, and intuition. It is conducted without any practical end in mind, although it may have unexpected results pointing to practical applications. The terms basic or fundamental indicate that, through theory generation, basic research provides the foundation for further, sometimes applied research (UT Dallas, 2012). Funding is neither an issue nor a factor of conducting a new study to determine the effectiveness of PIP's.

When speaking of a new direction it would be beneficial overall to conduct the study using a different organization other than NHA. As mentioned earlier during the findings of the survey results, a large portion of the responses dealt with PIP's being viewed negatively as a result of dilemmas in regards to NHA, NHA's management team, organizational structure, and their overall employee morale. Blindly knowing that so many underlying problems were factored in made the study biased in more ways than one.

Many of the responses were solely based upon the fact that NHA had many issues keeping employees from performing better regardless of PIP's or not. With over ninety percent of the responses being the same it is safe to say that a longitudinal approach pertaining to the research design or survey may be necessary to study the same subjects (employees and participants of PIP's) repeatedly over a period of time. Although, using another organization in place of NHA.

A New PIP Plan

A plan of action could include providing an overall survey to all employees whom will participate in the study determining their foundational background and overall view of the organization prior to providing the actual study to test for and research performance improvement. This survey would include questions such as those listed in Figure 1.6. This would be considered a pre-qualification survey to determine if the employee is positive, negative or neutral with the organization so minimal biasing factors will arise when the actual study is conducted and the survey questions are distributed.

The prequalification survey will be distributed to all of the employees under the false pretense that it is an organizational review survey. This survey will gain some input on how employees feel about the organization. It has been noted from previous research that employees like to feel important and give feedback; the second attempt with regards to researching PIP's will be conducted with more of a blind study format. PIP's will not be mentioned in the prequalification study. The results will determine which subjects will be chosen to move on to the actual PIP and performance improvement study.

The survey results were an important factor in determining if PIP's were beneficial or non-beneficial with less weight and focus on the overall organization. Although, for future research prior to and during the surveying of the subjects an overall research study will be done of the organization as well.

It was not only how the subjects viewed NHA that was an issue; but also what went unknown about NHA in terms of the organization and overall company morale, ethics and the code of conducts. Research was conducted in regards to the general makeup of NHA. However, for future research a very detailed research study will be conducted. This will actually look at all aspects of the chosen organization; again, with the notion of limiting or eliminating bias.

The importance of the organizational standpoint cannot be stressed enough in depth. For further research knowing what type of foundation the organization has is a number one priority. In the original study NHA was not researched in depth. There was no input from the employees regarding the organization, nor was there adequate research outside of what could be seen working within NHA. This is something that has to shift entirely for the new study to be successful in regards to providing useful information about PIP's.

For future research regardless of the chosen organization a detailed history and debriefing will be conducted from the bottom to the top of the organization. This will list all employees, employee duties, employee job titles, and employee rates of pay, all documentation within the HR files such as years of experience, evaluations, certifications and degrees.

Accounting information will be necessary; including the financial department as well as the payroll department will need to provide all necessary data. Information on all grants and loan documents will be necessary to determine what standards the organization has to abide by in order to maintain some of if not all of their funding's and accreditations. Even comparing and contrasting vision and mission statements to operational settings will be studied.

In short, the organizational behavior (OB) and all aspects of such will be under review and examined; unlike NHA. OB will also be included in the research breakdown in definition as well which will have a similar setup resembling the defining process of PIP's.

Developing Organizational Behavior (NHA)

Organizational Behavior (OB) is the study and application of knowledge about how people, individuals, and groups act in organizations (Pomsuwan, 2007).

It does this by taking a system approach. Meaning, it interprets individual's organization relationships in terms of the whole person, whole group, whole organization, and whole social system. Its purpose is to build better relationships by achieving human objectives, organizational objectives, and social objectives.

The organization's base rests on management's philosophy, values, vision and goals. This in turn drives the organizational culture which is composed of the formal organization, informal organization, and the social environment. The culture determines the type of leadership, communication, and group dynamics within the organization. The workers perceive this as the quality of work life which directs their degree of motivation. The final outcomes are performance, individual satisfaction, and personal growth and development. All these elements combine to build the model or framework that the organization operates from (Pomsuwan, 2007).

Table 2.1 The organizational behavior model details examples of structured OB.

There are four major models or frameworks that organizations operate out of, Autocratic, custodial, supportive, and collegial. Although there are four separate models, almost no organization operates exclusively in one (Pomsuwan, 2007).

There will usually be a predominate one, with one or more areas over-lapping in the other models. Model one, autocratic has its roots in the industrial revolution. The other three models begin to build on McGregor's Theory Y. They have each evolved over a period of time and there is no one that is better than the other three. The OB framework of the chosen organization will be determined and explained in depth as well for future the future research study. This was something that had not been performed during the first study with NHA.

Conclusion

In summation, it has been stated that overall the hypothesis of PIP's improving job performance was null and void. It is still unknown whether or not there is improvement or no difference. The data from the research study was biased in more ways than one due to a conflict of interest found with the employees of NHA. No useful information could be given about PIP's and it has been suggested that further research be done to determine whether or not PIP's improve or have no impact on job performance.

With further research it has also been determined that another organization be used, and a screening process be conducted on all employees. The employees will be chosen for the study based on their organizational responses, meaning how they feel about their organization. A complete history and background study will also be done on the organization prior to the actual PIP study to limit bias and underlying problems that cause the original study to be unsuccessful.

Adding this detailed information to a future study on PIP's using the same PIP survey, chances are the data will be more reliable and concrete facts and a solid assumption can be made on the hypothesis of whether PIP's have an effect negatively or positively on job performance.

Figure 1.6 Organizational Review Survey

1. Please state your gender.

○ Male

○ Female

2. Please state your age.

○ 18-23

○ 24-29

○ 30-35

○ 36-41

○ 42-46

○ 47-51

○ 52-57

○ 58-63

○ 64+

3. Please state your field.

○ Healthcare

○ Medical

○ Marketing

○ Agriculture

○ Transportation

○ Administration

○ Pharmaceuticals

○ Factory/Warehouse/Production

○ Data Entry

○ Clerical

○ Other

_____

4. How many years of experience do you have with your organization?

○ 0-3

○ 4-6

○ 7-10

○ 11-13

○ 14-17

○ 17+

5. Do you have any issues regarding your organization? If yes, explain.

○ Yes

○ No

_____

6. Do you have any issues regarding the management team within your organization? If yes, explain.

○ Yes

○ No

_____

7. Please give the best answer in regards to your work ethic?

○ High work ethic

○ Low work ethic

○ I don't have a work ethic

○ Work ethic has no role in what I do at work

○ What do you mean by work ethic?

8. Please give your overall rating of your organization in regards to morale, mission, vision, performance; basically it's operational functions.

○ Extremely Poor

○ Poor

○ Average

○ Above Average

○ Excellent

○ Excellent A+

○ No opinion/rating

○ I don't care

9. Does your organization offer incentives?

○ Yes

○ No

○ They don't care about us

10. How would you describe how you feel when you are at work? Choose <u>ONLY ONE</u>

○ I wish I was not at work.

○ I need a new job.

○ I apply for new jobs online all the time while at work.

○ I feel fine when at work, typical issues but that's with all organizations.

○ I dislike this company so much; I hate it.

○ Why am I still working here?

○ If I quit, can I make it without a job until I find a new one.

○ I love my job

○ Neutral "It is what it is"

○ I "cyberloaf" the day away, so I could care less what goes on at work.

    ***Cyberloaf=surfing the internet all day…

- If I click my heels 3 times maybe I will wake up at a new organization.
- This is not a job, this is He!! on earth.
- I just focus on my paycheck.
- I don't mind coming to work.
- This is more than my job; this is my career choice.
- I can't find anything better at the moment so this will suffice.
- I am completely satisfied at work.
- I would be satisfied…if I made more money.
- Words cannot explain how I feel when I am at work.
- My soul bleeds while working.
- Work is the leading cause of my stress, health issues and/or smoking.
- We have free Wi-Fi at work, I can Facebook and more; no worries.
- Other

If other selected, please detail below:

_____

Table 2.1 Models of Organizational Behavior

OB Model	Information Regarding Organizational Behavior
Model One: Autocratic	The basis of this model is power with a managerial orientation of authority. The employees in turn are oriented towards obedience and dependence on the boss. The employee need that is met is subsistence. The performance result is minimal.
Model Two: Custodial	The basis of this model is economic resources with a managerial orientation of money. The employees in turn are oriented towards security and benefits and dependence on the organization. The employee need that is met is security. The performance result is passive cooperation.
Model Three: Supportive	The basis of this model is leadership with a managerial orientation of support. The employees in turn are oriented towards job performance and participation. The employee need that is met is status and recognition. The performance result is awakened drives.
Model Four: Collegial	The basis of this model is partnership with a managerial orientation of teamwork. The employees in turn are oriented towards responsible behavior and self-discipline. The employee need that is met is self-actualization. The performance result is moderate enthusiasm.

References

ASTD. (2010). *Performance improvement*. Retrieved from

http://www.astd.org/communities/networks/performanceImprovement/

Brown, P. (1998). Technology and performance improvement: intellectual partners?. *Quality Progress*, *31*(4), 69.

Corporate Executive Board. (2004). *The use of competencies in performance management programs*. Informally published manuscript, Business, Harvard University, Cambridge, MA. Retrieved from http://www.harvard.edu

Cummings, T.G., & Worley, C.G. (2008). *Organization development & change*. Mason, OH: Cengage Learning.

Daft, R. L. (2007). *Organization theory and design*. (9 ed.). Mason: South-Western, a part of Cengage Learning.

Department of Public Safety. (2011). *Developing a performance improvement program*. Retrieved from website:

http://www.publicsafety.ohio.gov/links/ems_pim_manual.pdf

Dessler, G. (2008). *Human resource management*. (11 ed.). Upper Saddle River: Pearson Prentice hall.

Farnsworth, T. (1979). How to develop yourself. *Management today*, Retrieved from http://ezproxy.arbor.edu:80/login?url=http://search.proquest.com.ezproxy.arbor.edu/docview/214790209?accountid=13398

FAS Human Resources. (2011, April). *FAS performance management guidelines.* Retrieved from http://www.hr.fas.harvard.edu/icb/icb.do?keyword=k69588&pageid=icb.page345525

Health Resources and Service Administration. (2010). *340B information guide.* Retrieve from http://www.hrsa.gov/opa/introduction.htm

Indiana State University. (2012). *Performance improvement plan.* Retrieved from http://www.indiana.edu/~uhrs/training/ca/performance.html

International Society for Performance Improvement. (2011). *Bringing performance techniques to your managers and supervisors.* Retrieved from http://ww.ispi.org

Luoma, M, & Voltero, L. (2011). *The Prime II Project.* Retrieved from http://www.prime2.org

Mark Crowell Consulting. (2008). *Performance improvement programs.* Retrieved from http://markcrowell.com

Michigan State University. (2012, January). *Performance improvement plan.* Retrieved from http://www.hr.msu.edu/performance/supportstaff/staffperformance_docs/PIP.pdf

N. Balakrishnan, Johnson, N.L., S. Koltz. (1994) Continuous Univariate Distributions (Second Ed., Vol.1.1, Chapter 18). John Willey and Sons.

Neighborhood Health Association. (2009). *Mission and vision statement.* Retrieved from http://www.nhainc.org/

Pomsuwan, S. (2007). *Organizational behavior: Theories and concepts*. Informally published manuscript, Business Department, Bangkok International University, Bangkok 10110, Thailand. Retrieved from http://bupress.bu.ac.th/ebook/mba/ba511_Suthinan.pdf

Reitmeier, S. (2005, December). *Performance improvement program description*. Retrieved fromhttp://www.ewashtenaw.org/government/departments/cmhpsm/committees/performance improvement/PI Comm/pi_prog_dscrp_06_07

Society for Human Resource Management (2010, November 16). *Management by objectives*. Retrieved from http://www.shrm.org.

Texas Medical Association. (2011). *Performance improvement programs*. Retrieved from http://www.texmed.org/Performance_Improvement_Programs.aspx

UT Dallas. (2012, February 24). *Performance improvement plan*. Retrieved from http://www.utdallas.edu/hrm/er/pm/improvementplans

Young, J. (1994). Mead: Performance improvement program on track. In *Pulp and Paper* San Francisco: Risi Inc.

Zikmund, W. G., Babin, B. J., Carr, J. C., & Griffin, M. (2010). *Business research methods*. (8 ed.). Mason: South-Western Cengage Learning.

Appendix A

Thesis and Problem Statement

Problem: Many organizations do not participate in Performance Improvement Programs and the reason depends on whether or not they are beneficial or non beneficial to the organization.

Thesis: Performance Improvement Programs & PIP's Effect's On Job Performance.

Appendix B

Master's Thesis Topic Proposal

Name: Nikki Giovanni Barnett   Group: MOD T-14   Date: April 20, 2012

Respond to the following questions. Strive for complete, yet concise, statements.

1. Problem Statement (this can take the form of a statement or question and should include where the problem is found, major elements or variables involved, and the population affected).

This proposal asks the question do Performance Improvement Programs (PIP's) have an effect on job performance. PIP's supposedly better the place of employment, employees, management and overall organizational morale. PIP's are said to help eliminate symptoms within an organization. Many organizations take part in PIP's but for this thesis the problem lies within Neighborhood Health Association (NHA). The elements involved are the employees within NHA and the effects of PIP's when involving job performance when related to the employees.

2. What is your personal involvement with the problem, and to what degree do you have control over the situation? (Please note your job title and how many years you have been with the company.)

I am an employee with NHA. Currently I am the Acting Pharmacy Manager and have been for the past eight months. I have been employed with NHA since July 2010. As far as my control over the situation; I do have direct contact with the CEO and CFO and my input is highly considered when trying to remedy a problem. Therefore, if I believe that PIP's will help or hinder NHA this feedback will be considered amongst the rest of upper management and a decision will be made as to how NHA can remedy job performance problems, and or whether or not PIP's are necessary.

3. On the basis of your problem analysis, what are your explanations and assumptions regarding the cause(s) of this problem?

I am an employee with NHA. Currently I am the Acting Pharmacy Manager and have been for the past eight months. I have been employed with NHA since July 2010. As far as my control over the situation; I do have direct contact with the CEO and CFO and my input is highly considered when trying to remedy a problem. Therefore, if I believe that PIP's will help or hinder NHA this feedback will be considered amongst the rest of upper management and a decision will be made as to how NHA can remedy job performance problems, and or whether or not PIP's are necessary.

I actually believe that if more employees were involved in PIP's the overall job performance would increase for the better. I do not feel that many employees give a minimal thirty percent let alone one hundred percent when it comes to job performance. Most employees are just there for a paycheck. PIP's in my opinion help identify weaknesses and turn them into strengths. This is what I would like to attempt to prove from my thesis.

4. Specifically, in what practical ways will the situation improve if the problem is solved? How will your organization benefit?

The overall improvement to come from the thesis is the generalization that providing PIP's to employees will in turn improve job performance in some way, thus improve the overall morale of NHA. The company as whole will benefit as a result. Some of NHA's major grants focus on quality of care and job performance being that NHA is a 340b non-profit organization. The employee will benefit as well being able to enhance skills for themselves currently and for the future within or outside of NHA.

APPROVAL:

Thesis Professor: _____ Date: _____

Site Contact: _____ Date: 6-14-12

Appendix C

Reflections

This appendix is a discussion of my personal thoughts reflected through my project thesis. It indirectly reflects my present thought process through my educational trials and tribulations nearing the completion of the Spring Arbor University MSM program. It also analyzes and summarizes my feelings, learning outcomes and my mental state of self-being from initiation of the project thesis to the conclusion.

My reflection commonly describes my conceptualization and concrete beliefs as a student as well as a soon to be graduate. This project thesis has questions within itself such as; what generalized learning can be used for researchers and or other research situations, expected and unexpected outcomes and what design and intellectual techniques I used during my research analysis. This appendix will conclude my thesis project by detailing my overall career learning's. A concluding summary of my reflections, also known as my experiences with this project thesis as well as my college experience in the MSM program in direct relations to my employer at the time my thesis was written, my personal and social activities as well as my life in broad-spectrum; all similarities and differences will be noted.

My personal thoughts about my 273.50 hours spent on my project thesis are minimal due to the fact that words cannot express my true feelings. I do believe that this project thesis has helped develop, maintain and critique my writing technique and style overall. This project has improved my thinking ability and it has made me more developed and grounded as an individual within my personal and professional life. On the other hand my thesis project has indirectly reassured many of my world views in relation to employers. It has shown me that there are still many employers whom do not stand behind their vision and or mission and they have minimal regards to their employees. Yet and still they expect so much from these underpaid overworked individuals.

When I began my project thesis I gained the insight from one of my professors as to what I should study. Performance improvement seemed to be an issue at the time at NHA so we went from there. What I can say is from the point where I began my thesis I had a different view of my employer. I honestly thought I had a semi-decent place to work. By the time I received all of my survey results; comments and emails, I had a completely new look on NHA. I actually became disgusted and wish I would have done more research on the company prior to presenting the employers with the surveys.

I was told by the CEO that I was a rock, the glue that held the pharmacy department together. At the time I was the only employee left. When everyone else quit or was terminated for various reasons in my department I did not opt to leave. I decided to be loyal. I decided to stay. Not for myself or NHA but for the patients. I worked double shifts without any extra incentives or staff for 8 months. I did this faithfully never late, no call offs. I even rescheduled medical appointments and skipped vacation days until we finally had adequate staffing again. About a year and a half later (present day) I decided to leave the company because I gained my first instructing position at college. I provided NHA with a notice and the next day, they attempted to fire me.

From that point forward I realized that in this world loyalty means nothing to employers. If you choose to be that hard dedicated worker with ethics and morale do it for yourself and your self-worth. Don't do it for the employer because you may feel like you mean nothing to them in the end. I can honestly say I did it for myself and I have no regrets I know my own self worth. My leaving NHA was their lost and obviously my blessing. After reading my survey results and what employees had to say about the company. I have to honestly say I was blind to the employee treatment being in a separate department.

From a student point of view, I am very proud of having accomplished a project thesis a second time. When I began this program, I knew a thesis was required for graduation and I had no problem with writing a seventy page document again having succeeded the first time through. I have come a long way as a writer as I enjoy writing and improving my skills, techniques and style. Being able to notice a difference in my own writing and the grading of my assignments shows that my learning abilities and cognitive skills have advanced as well.

Given an entire year to complete the project thesis; the hardest part is staying on task. When we as a cohort came down to the final months of class it was very troubling listening to my fellow classmates state that they were behind or they were not going to be finished at the same time as myself. I have empathy for them but at the same time, it is a master's level program. Hard work is a requirement of a master's level program. I recall repeatedly, just as with my undergrad degree in the MOD program on numerous occasions various instructors stating *"Do not fall behind"*.

Just as the MOD program our instructors made it very clear that staying on task is detrimental to this project thesis and once behind it would be difficult to regain a current state physically and mentally. I myself chose to listen. Despite any and all problems in my life I always put forth some effort and managed to turn in some type of completed chapter on the due date. I am assuming this is not one of those *"I told you so"* moments; this is a moment of truth for a lot of individuals in my class. I do hope and pray that we all walk together on graduation day.

My project thesis evolved from countless hours of time and effort. This project thesis also better helped me understand what is meant by a hypothesis and what can come from a hypothesis. This also was the first time I ever had a null and void hypothesis on a project due to biased data in all my years of college.

When concerning other researchers or situations, I would actually suggest utilizing this same design if and when the study is repeated. The easiest way to see results is to conduct surveys and do a compare and contrast study using the process of elimination to determine where major flaws and limitations rest. I myself like research, so I feel that the more surveys conducted the better the outcomes. Feedback of any kind is always useful. On the other hand I would give a suggestion to future researchers; research the organization in depth before choosing your survey subjects. A possible burn out risk is not a factor with this thesis from my standpoint.

Describing my conceptualization and concrete beliefs as a student as well as a soon to be graduate; I feel so accomplished at this moment in my life this being my second thesis as I prepare for my doctorate program God willing I get accepted. I am a believer that when one door shuts another door opens. I did indeed have to face an ethical dilemma with NHA during the course of the MSM program just as I did with the MOD program. But at the same time while NHA shunned me, my new employer welcomed me and I became the Lead Instructor of the program within the first week of my employment.

Again, I was beginning to doubt myself as an employee, trying to find faults, flaws and imperfections within myself of any sort to relate to NHA's negative actions. I then asked many others who told me, it wasn't me; I give one hundred percent if not more with all things. My director at my current place of employment reassured me that it was indeed them and they deserve whatever may come to them. I had to recapture my sound state of mind and remind myself that I am an overachiever. I put forth my best efforts with any and everything I do, regardless of how monotonous or substantial the task may be. Based upon NHA's actions and previous experiences with employers I am still trying to eliminate employers making me doubt my self-worth.

My current abilities in MSM reside with my higher power and SAU for helping develop my skills. I am graduating from the MSM program with a positive outlook that I have indeed learned multiple key aspects from this program and I have utilized many of them professionally and personally. Again, I decided to continue my education and begin my Doctorate program this fall if I am accepted, or shall I say God willing.

Now as an effect of finding what I like to do in life, I currently accomplished that goal with my first instructing position. I am the Lead Instructor for the Pharmacy Technician Program at Ross College. I always wanted to give back my gained knowledge and teach. Now I am setting my goal toward teaching at a major university. I dream of Harvard University but I will settle for the University of Michigan or the University of

Toledo. I too would like to instruct students and tell them that life is what they make of it. I want students to know that college is very necessary for any type of progression in life.

I believe that I have touched on all aspects required of this reflection. Now I would like to use the remainder of my appendix to touch base on a few aspects of my personal life reflecting upon my studies at SAU in the MSM program. I am once again bothered by something our Christian university has done. This time I had to withdraw from my class and sign up for an online session due to a instructor whom was irrational with his comments and ways. Please SAU if you want to give us arrogant professors please do so in the beginning of the module. Do not wait until I last few classes when we have the most stress to bring upon the most troublesome professor I have ever came across in all my years of college.

My cohort is a cohort with many faces. Another thing I did not like is how the older members in my cohort make the younger members feel uneasy. It must be rare for adult learning to consist of individuals in their twenties and early thirties. It's almost a bit of age discrimination if you ask my honest opinion. I give all due credit to the instructors, with all belief in my higher power, I too hope to be a member of the SAU faculty. The instructors deal with so much, and being able to hold a professional composure is phenomenal in my eyesight when dealing with various personality types.

As I near the end of my reflections I can honestly say that it has been a very interesting journey. I have graduated from college four times previously and this by far is my most memorable completion of a program. There were many first time experiences for myself and preparing for the Doctorate program I am sure there will be many more.

SAU was the first college where I had ever felt empathy toward other student's situations, ethical dilemmas and life's trials and tribulations in general. SAU was the first college where I ever disclosed close and personal facts and information with a cohort as a group or with individual students. SAU is the first college where I have given my last anything to help a fellow classmate. SAU is the first college where we eat and pray together as a family. SAU is the first college where I conducted a group assignment in class through the communicational lines of face book. SAU is the first college where I gained motivation from face book. SAU is the first college for prayers to specifically go out to my fellow classmates; for completion of all their assignments and necessary requirements for November 2012's MSM graduation ceremony. SAU is the first college I attended that I actually didn't mind writing a project thesis for. SAU is the first college that I lost a fellow classmate, his wife, and son due to a tornado in Ohio (RIP Ryan Walters). Lastly, SAU is the first college that has motivated me to never stop learning and continue to strive for my doctorate.

In conclusion, from starting with *Graduate Orientation* and ending with *Ethical Issues* in attendance at SAU, the one thing I am graduating with is the respect of oneself and the respect of others. Congratulations to all SAU graduates including myself and good luck to all students, staff and faculty with any aspect of life's journey. I pray that our higher power be with all SAU beings including family and friends before and after graduation.

www.ingramcontent.com/pod-product-compliance
Lightning Source LLC
Chambersburg PA
CBHW050740180526
45159CB00003B/1293